Treasure Under Pressure

A Diamond Rising from Pearls and Perseverance

Treasure Under Pressure
A Diamond Rising from Pearls and Perseverance

Written and Lived By: Elaine Moody

Treasure Under Pressure: A Diamond Rising from Pearls and Perseverance

Copyright © 2025 by Elaine Moody

All rights reserved. Aside from brief passages in a published review, no part of this book may be reproduced or transmitted in any form or by any means - electronic, mechanical, photocopy, recording, scanning or any other technologies known or later developed, without written permission from the author, Elaine Moody.

Ignited Ink 717 LLC

Houston, TX

Cover Design: EbonyRose Smith of Ignited Ink 717 LLC

Categories: Self-Help/Professional Development

Elaine Moody is available for keynotes, panels, book talks, and workshops.

Discounts for bulk purchases of 25 books or more are available.

Visit IgnitedInk717.com to learn more and place an order.

For reprint permission, write to IgnitedInk717@gmail.com

ISBN (PRINT): 979-8-9909403-8-3

ISBN (EBOOK): 979-8-9909403-6-9

Printed in the United States of America

Dedication

This book is affectionately dedicated to my precious mother, Ms. Artice J. Johnson, whose dedicated commitment and sacrifices made my childhood one of cherished memories.

My gracious aunt, Mrs. Mildred "Lady J" Johnson, and my entrepreneurial grandparents, Mr. and Mrs. Lonnie and Virginia Paley, whose influence has significantly shaped my life.

My children Clifton, Chanel, Jakari, and Amber continue to inspire me to strive for
excellence as I witness their successes.

My encouragement came from my husband, William, as well as from my colleagues
and various business organizations that welcomed me into their groups.

Lastly, for all those who continue to embrace their uniqueness and consistently
strive for greatness.

Table of Contents

Positive Thinking	Ch1	PG 001
Endurance	Ch2	PG 013
Affirmation	Ch3	PG 038
Reassurance	Ch4	PG 052
Living for a Legacy	Ch5	PG 069
Success	Ch6	PG 084

Bonus

Treasure — PG 096

Under Pressure — PG 104

Positive Thinking

"I can do all things through Jesus Christ who strengthens me."
Philippians 4:13 (KJV)

Just Keep Believing

With courage and resilience, I've emerged from my shell,
With a compelling and inspirational story to tell
When the noble attributes of faith and trust intertwine
My beliefs strengthened, and my paths redefined.
Be assured, trials and tribulations didn't break me
For here I stand, claiming my season of prosperity
Just Keep Believing.

Stay encouraged and focused on your purpose and plan
Do you know who holds the future in their hand?
Always remember, faith is not just a mere decree,
It's a beacon of light guiding you to see all the possibilities.
Just Keep Believing

Like diamonds and pearls that glisten and gleam
So are the virtues of confidence, commitment, and self-esteem
I'm claiming this is my season to fulfill my destiny
I pledge to create more than just material wealth for my family legacy.
Just keep believing.

In my early childhood, my grandfather, Mr. Lonnie Paley (my mom's father), described me as "the quiet one" because I preferred being reserved and keeping my thoughts to myself. My mind was constantly analyzing the strategies he initiated to earn respect and a commendable reputation in the community. It was captivating to witness how proficiently he conducted transactions with his rental properties and managed the neighborhood grocery store. I realized later that this environment served as the backdrop to my career in real estate and business administration/management. My childhood was very sheltered and focused on school and church; however, I desired the acceptance and camaraderie of others.

My weekend routine included playing jacks on our front porch with my sisters Elyse and Angela and my friend Jerrilyn "Jerri," who lived a few houses down and is now deceased. Treasured moments of close connection with my two friends, Linda, who is still in my life, and Mercury, now deceased, provided a sense of value that enriched my life in countless ways. Their support, honesty, laughter, and companionship gave me a feeling of belonging.

As I matured, the pressure of trying to fit in with other girls, groups, and organizations began to stress me out. Pondering what makes people popular compelled me to take an honest look at my attributes and shortcomings. I began by compiling a list of my positive traits—commitment, creativity, determination, and respect—that have been deep-rooted in me since my youth. I was determined to become a successful businesswoman committed to creating a positive impact through exemplary service. The unexpected status of becoming a single parent shifted my priorities to focus on my children. I juggled jobs while supporting my kids in school activities but managed to attend night classes for several years.

Happy feelings come over me when I think about the times my daughter, Chanel, and I walked the halls of the Jesse H. Jones School of Business at Texas Southern University together. She was studying for her master's degree in business administration, and I was studying for my bachelor's degree in business administration. The last class I needed to complete for graduation was taught by Professor Tai, one of the toughest professors in the School of Business. He was known for requiring rigorous studies and giving complex exams. I had no alternative but to register for his class since it was the only one that fit my schedule. My desire to graduate exceeded my fear of failure, so I reluctantly registered for the class.

    I dealt with the stress of struggling with his complicated calculus methods and language barriers. To overcome this, I recorded and reviewed all the lectures and listened to them after every class. This intensive study resulted in sleepless nights and weight loss. The practice of prayer was constant throughout every assignment and exam during the semester. One evening, I was stunned and speechless as he called my name for making the highest score on the exam. It gave me a feeling of pride and nervousness at the same time. All the students looked at me with the hope that I would help them study. At the end of the course, I received an email from Professor Tai congratulating me for passing the class and persevering. My self-confidence went "through the roof."

After those long, hard years of work and sacrifice, the reward was beyond my expectations. My first academic achievement, an associate's degree in social studies (cum laude) from North Harris Community College, was shared with my oldest son, Clifton, as he earned his bachelor's degree in music from The University of Texas-Austin, and my younger son, Jakari, as he earned his high school diploma from Eisenhower High School. My second academic achievement, a Bachelor of Arts degree from Texas Southern University in business administration/management, was shared with my younger daughter Amber who graduated magna cum laude from Howard University with a major in English and a scholarship to Southwestern School of Law in San Diego, California. I still get emotional when I look at the cap and gown pictures from each ceremony. A thought of gratefulness humbled me as I thought, "How many parents get the opportunity to study and graduate with their kids?"

I compiled another list of my shortcomings, which included procrastination, being overly sensitive to negative comments, and ignoring discerning instincts. It required extensive self-reflection to discover my reasons for procrastinating on certain goals. The most significant factor was becoming complacent; the other was anticipating the work involved. One of my most notable experiences with procrastination stemmed from launching a project related to my vision for my mother's property. My goal was to construct a multifamily dwelling to serve as a rental property, continuing the legacy started by my grandfather.

At first, it seemed like an unattainable goal, but after listening to a panel of investors present various types of funding, I gained a new perspective. After properly filing a Deed of Trust and obtaining a survey, I began a step-by-step plan to acquire appraisals and possibly partner with a builder to assist with permits, engineering blueprints, and other requirements needed for a hard money loan to succeed in this large endeavor.

In exploring the area of oversensitivity and disregarding discernment, a deeper evaluation revealed my tendency to seek acceptance from others, avoid conflict, and be a "people pleaser." I don't remember when it happened, but an epiphany occurred and a realization that my priority should be doing what is pleasing to God and nurturing my spiritual relationship with him.

"Blessed are the peacemakers, for they will be called the children of God"

Matthew 5:9 (NIV)

I experienced discouraging responses in an atmosphere that should have been supportive. My genuine efforts to arrive early and eagerly volunteer my services resulted in whispered comments about my sincerity, suggesting my motive was to gain attention. Reflecting on my blessed testimonies helped me regain a positive outlook that renewed my sense of self-worth. I recognized that my primary goal is to embody a virtuous character and contribute quality service in all I do.

There's a reality in understanding that you will never please everyone. Instead of trying to meet everyone's expectations, stay true to your own values and gravitate toward those who genuinely appreciate you. This approach helps reduce unnecessary stress and anxiety. Cultivate a positive mindset by surrounding yourself with uplifting influences—whether through inspirational songs, scriptures, films, creating vision boards, or engaging in creative outlets like designing. Seek guidance from mentors who exemplify great character and allow their wisdom to shape your growth. This focus on authenticity and self-care will lead to a more fulfilling and peaceful life.

Diamond Moment

Embracing a positive mindset will develop constructive actions and visionary outcomes.

Father and Mother

Endurance

"But he that shall endure unto the end, the same shall be saved."
Matthew 24:13 (KJV)

Endurance can be defined by perseverance and resilience, enabling one to persist through prolonged difficulties and challenges. It demonstrates stamina in the face of adversity and emphasizes how determination and steadfastness influence one's decisions in life.

Getting Past the Grief

Life is full of unexpected situations that can be exciting and inspiring, while others are sorrowful and depressing. The death of a loved one, abuse (both physically and mentally), critical health conditions, and lack of finances are among the most serious events that create despair. Maslow's Hierarchy of Needs explains that individuals must satisfy lower-level needs (physiological and safety needs) before focusing on higher-level needs such as self-esteem and self-actualization. Endurance plays a major role in this process.

Persevering and enduring difficult times can be extremely challenging and leave permanent scars of anxiety, stress, and depression. The healing process may take time, patience, and support from others. It's almost certain that everyone is likely to encounter some form of grief in their lifetime.

The deepest period of grief in my life was the death of my mother. She was my closest friend, and we talked daily. Some thought she was my older sister. After starting my family, I continued visiting my grandparents and mother on Sundays after church since they only lived a block away. One Sunday, we talked at the dining room table, and she shared some of her health problems. The following night, when the phone rang, she whispered in a strained voice, "Lanie, I'm sick." My immediate reactions were shock, fear, and tears, followed by prayer. After that, adrenaline kicked in, giving me the strength to contact my sister Elyse to inform her about the situation.

When Elyse arrived at the house, it was obvious that Mama needed to be transported to the hospital in an ambulance for emergency surgery. It felt like we were in a bad dream when the doctors told us our mother had a large mass on her colon and had been diagnosed with Stage 4 cancer. They proceeded to tell us she had a life expectancy of approximately five years with the help of radiation and chemotherapy. Our heart-to-heart talks were precious and sometimes so painful that only the grace of God allowed me to endure. As my mother confessed the fear of dying and requested that my children never forget her, she explained that she was not worried about her eternal destination. To this day, those words have had the most profound impact on me.

Three months later, in May 1983, my mother transitioned, just two weeks after my son Jakari was born. Amid my grief, I struggled with depression and postpartum challenges while trying to do my best to fulfill my role as a wife, mother, and employee. As time passed, my mother's cherished memories served as a tribute, validating that her sacrifices were not in vain. The commitment to do my best in all endeavors inspired me to embark on my personal development journey.

Conquering sad emotions one day at a time allows you to adjust gradually to your new situation. Inspirational support from family and friends is priceless because it builds trusting relationships that allow you to share your thoughts. The following scripture read at my mother's homegoing service gave me solace.

"And God will wipe away all tears from their eyes; and there shall be no more death, neither sorrow, neither shall there be any more pain; for the former things are passed away."

Revelations 21:4 (KJV)

Strength and Stamina

Endurance is essential for completing goal-oriented activities, such as finishing a race physically and mentally. Organizations like the March of Dimes and Susan G. Komen resonate with me because I can relate to their cause. Participating in the annual 5K and 10K walks and runs gave me the opportunity to interact with thousands of individuals who shared the same objectives. Over time, my involvement in these charity runs became a cherished part of our family Thanksgiving tradition. My daughter, Chanel, an enthusiastic marathon runner, was instrumental in organizing the participation of myself, my son Clifton, my daughter Amber, and herself in the "Turkey Trott," held in the Houston, Texas Galleria area for over 13 years.

At the beginning of one race, I felt energetic and excited; however, around the fourth or fifth mile, fatigue began to take over. When gazing through the crowded sidelines, there were several groups, including spectators, waving their hands and holding up signs of encouragement. There were also volunteers handing out water and cheerleaders chanting, "You can do it," and "Just keep going;" this gave me the surge of energy I needed to cross the finish line and receive my medal. This kind of motivation can serve as a powerful tool during challenging situations when goals seem unattainable. With faith, positive affirmations and consistently moving forward, you can overcome obstacles and claim success.

Maintaining Resilience in the Midst of Mistreatment

Many people experience some form of abuse or mistreatment at various points in their lives. This abuse can manifest as physical acts such as assault, sexual harassment, or even shootings, which can be fatal. Additionally, psychological abuse—such as insults, threats, slander, cyberbullying, harassment, and intimidation—can cause lasting harm. An abusive childhood and excessive use of alcohol and drugs can also lead to behaviors that perpetuate the mistreatment of others. A good question to ask yourself when trying to bounce back from a negative experience is: "What steps can I take to regain my self-worth and empowerment?" A helpful solution is to bring awareness to the situation.

I have deep admiration for Dr. Cherrye Vasquez, who advocates against child bullying through her impactful series of books, including *Teacher, Teacher Can't You See*, *Clique, Clique, STOP*, and *No Tildes on Tuesday*. These and other similar publications illustrate how children try to reach out for help when encountering bullies. Vasquez's books are also a great resource for teachers, parents, daycare workers, and others by helping them identify warning signs and develop strategies to assist those in need. Can you imagine being a child harassed by a bully and afraid to tell someone?

Throughout my early school years, I endured constant teasing about my extra slim figure and the gap in my front teeth. This fostered feelings of inferiority, low self-esteem, and insecurity in me. The neighborhood kids teased me and my sisters about our protective environment and limited socialization.

As I grew older, situations of mistreatment occurred on a higher level. These instances occurred both in the workplace and in relationships, compounded by the burden of health challenges, which required endurance and positive thinking. Resolving these situations involved a systematic approach, including analyzing problems and implementing practical solutions, which cultivated a feeling of maturity.

As a young adult, I encountered unfair treatment during my career in corporate America. Dealing with this injustice became frustrating and almost to the point of an emotional breakdown. There was so much backstabbing, jealousy, and rudeness that turning to God became the only source of solace that saved my sanity. The recurring pattern of training new employees and then watching them advance beyond me was depressing. Upon finally receiving a leadership position, new challenges of subtle racial undertones developed.

During one of my evaluations, the department manager, an African American male, informed me of the high marks earned in all categories. To my surprise, the next day was a different story when I was summoned into his office, greeted with a solemn face, and informed of a lower evaluation. The discernment deep inside me knew where this change of decision came from; however, the feelings of shock and dismay distracted me from taking the appropriate actions to address this injustice. Have you ever tried to console yourself and endure mistreatment by adopting a grateful mindset and thinking, "Well, at least I have a job?" I have, but my situation worsened, and I eventually had to change jobs.

A similar situation occurred to me again at a different job. It felt like déjà vu. This time, I learned how to utilize organizational protocols efficiently by meticulously documenting questionable situations, researching employee rights, and reaching out to representatives who could ensure the enforcement of both my rights and the rights of my colleagues. Even though my problem was temporarily resolved, my actions helped other employees who were also mistreated. Refining your self-worth through persevering challenges is similar to how diamonds and pearls become valuable through strenuous processes. Both involve enduring pressure that ultimately leads to resilience and value.

Enduring Bonds Produce Timeless Relationships

"Love does not delight in evil but rejoices with the truth. It always protects, always trusts, always hopes, always perseveres."

1 Corinthians 13:6-7 (NIV)

Enduring relationships are more precious than diamonds and pearls, yielding the radiance of time-tested bonds. Some of my most treasured moments of the close connection with my two childhood friends, Linda, with whom I've shared over 60 years, and Mercury, who is now deceased, provide a sense of value that enriched my life in countless ways. Their support, honesty, laughter, and companionship provided me with a deep sense of belonging. Having friends who have stood by you for over 60 years is a gift—an enduring testament to the strength of timeless connections with loyalty and love. A friendship that evolves into marriage between young couples can provide a unique and solid foundation for a lasting relationship. Even when faced with unforeseen challenges, their bond remains strong due to their shared history.

Marriage is a treasured milestone symbolizing the start of a shared journey filled with love, growth, and enduring partnership. My decision to marry Mr. Johnny R. Croomes Jr. right after high school led to significant changes. As newlyweds, we quickly experienced distance when he was deployed for basic training out of state while I began my studies at Texas Southern University. After basic training and my freshman semester, we relocated to Clarksville, Tennessee, where my son Clifton Croomes was born—a bicentennial baby. Despite our shared dreams and responsibilities, his new assignment in Germany and my choice to remain a parent in the United States strained our relationship, and we ultimately grew apart. Upon completing his enlisted term, we discovered our personalities were no longer compatible, leading us to the decision to divorce. Even though we have both remarried and have kids, we still respect each other.

After marrying Mr. William G. Moody a few years later, a new phase of my life unfolded, blessing me with three adorable children: Chanel, Jakari, and Amber. Despite the joy of our growing family and many accomplishments, such as moving into a prosperous neighborhood with great schools, significant challenges emerged in our relationship, including frequent arguments, trust issues, and poor financial decisions. Though I remained determined to maintain a positive outlook and believed perseverance would lead to improvement, I eventually recognized that positive personal changes were necessary to preserve our relationship.

Can you imagine how difficult it is for a mother of four to face divorce for the second time? The overwhelming stress, tormented nightmares, and unhealthy environment for the kids led me to make the difficult decision to move out and pursue a divorce. That's when my greatest transformation began. Fueling my faith with scriptures combined with the practice of prayer and supplication transformed my life.

A comforting home eradicates stress, promotes positive thinking, and cultivates a nurturing atmosphere. Maintaining mental health should be an utmost priority. Establishing a comfortable and positive environment was essential for me in navigating challenging obstacles and maintaining a productive co-parenting relationship. After many years, the personal growth we both experienced enabled us to remarry and establish a stronger, more resilient union. By actively engaging in self-improvement during challenging times in our relationship, we developed a deeper and more resilient bond. This strengthened our relationship and allowed us to withstand future challenges.

Health is the New Wealth

Have you ever contemplated how your physical and mental wellness might be the key to achieving higher financial success? Maslow's hierarchy of needs categorizes health, safety, and security as the second level of the pyramid because, after the basic physiological needs (food, water, and shelter), the next priority is feeling safe and secure. This involves physical safety, health, well-being, and financial and emotional safety.

Following the birth of my second child, Chanel, I was diagnosed with hyperthyroidism, which meant my body was producing excessive thyroid hormones. At the time, I didn't need medication or special dieting. However, about ten years ago, my condition changed from hyperthyroidism to hypothyroidism, resulting in decreased production of thyroid hormones. This seemed to trigger a series of health problems, including rheumatoid arthritis, a damaged rotator cuff, and borderline diabetes. As a result, I needed multiple daily prescriptions and dietary management. The possibility of developing diabetes frightened me, having witnessed the challenges that my father, grandmother, and other family members on my father's side endured.

Understanding the importance of health awareness is essential to personal growth. Participating in health seminars, attending presentations, reading health pamphlets, and consulting with nutritionists have provided valuable strategies personalized to my individual needs. Regular gym workouts, healthier foods, and yoga have contributed to a positive mindset regarding my physical well-being.

My gym experience begins as I enter the building in my fashionable workout attire, carrying my water bottle. I scan my QR code at the front desk and make my way through the aisle to select the best cardio equipment. The atmosphere is energetic and upbeat, with everyone laser-focused on their fitness routine. As I begin my workout, headphones snugly on, I immerse myself in motivational material that energizes my concentration and drive. Above the rows of weight machines, a line of TVs stretches across the upper border of the gym, displaying a variety of programs. While my eyes occasionally glance at the screens, my attention remains anchored on the powerful messages in my ears. One of the audiobooks I listen to is *The Disrupters* by the renowned minister T.D. Jakes. This book sheds light on the pathway to unleashing disruptive thinking, providing the wisdom and practical skills we need to transform our most promising ideas from vision to reality.

Eating healthy supports endurance by providing essential nutrients and energy to sustain physical and mental performance. My dietary journey has developed into a vibrant adventure where creativity and self-discipline converge. Integrating nutritional knowledge, taste preferences, and inspiration from role models has helped me achieve my personal health goals. My daughter Chanel is my most cherished role model because of her 130-lb weight loss journey. Her testimony validates perseverance.

"But we have this treasure in earthen vessels, that the excellency of the power may be of God and not of us."

- 2 Corinthians 4:7 (KJV)

"What? Know ye not that your body is the temple of the Holy Ghost which is in you, which ye have of God, and ye are not your own? For ye are bought with a price:

therefore glorify God in your body, and in your spirit, which is God's." - 1 Corinthians 6:19-20 (KJV)

The pandemic strengthened our endurance by forcing people to adapt to unprecedented challenges and uncertainties. As of March 2020, our nation experienced a shift in priorities that tested our resilience and ability to cope with disruptions of daily life, which included the government imposing a stay-at-home order. Stores, restaurants, educational institutions, and sporting events operated virtually or offered curbside services for approximately two years. During this time, society exhibited creativity and adaptability by utilizing technology such as Zoom meetings and other innovative services such as online food delivery. This period of adversity encouraged mental fortitude, flexibility, and problem-solving skills that enhanced our capacity to endure difficulties. My contribution was designing fashionably useful masks for family and friends.

Financial Fortitude

Financial fortitude is similar to the endurance a person practices in managing money matters. The main goal of organizing finances is to efficiently handle your income by allocating funds to accomplish both short-term and long-term objectives. As an acknowledged baby boomer, it's vital to prioritize my preparation for retirement. My early exposure to financial products during my banking career taught me to invest in savings bonds, IRAs, and other long-term investments, which enabled me to acquire funds to purchase high-yielding certificates of deposit. Pursuing wise investments while avoiding frivolous expenses is the foundation for achieving a prosperous financial future.

A good strategy for me involves allocating at least 10% of my paycheck to tithing, 10% to savings, and 80% to financial obligations and necessities. I introduced my kids to financial literacy at an early age by opening savings accounts for them and teaching them to understand and manage them.

This gave them first-hand exposure to how consistent deposits can increase the funds in their account.

Implementing smart financial practices allowed me to endure the struggles as a single parent. My budget for food and clothing was carefully allocated in such a way as to engage them in an exciting experience. We went to the park for picnics and shopped at discount food stores that sold their favorite specialty items. If anyone remembers the Fire Sale in downtown Houston, they'd remember the independent vendors lining the streets (near what is now the Toyota Center and Minute Maid Park), selling tapes and various items. This proved that precious moments can be created without a substantial amount of money. The excitement my kids displayed when anticipating our shopping routine reminds me of the shopping trips with my mother. We would ride the bus downtown, starting at one end of Main Street and finishing at the other. The Layaway department was a great asset to us when shopping for school clothes or at Christmas.

When managing finances, especially as a single parent, it's important to remember that you don't need to spend a lot of money to create meaningful experiences with your children. Finding joy in simple, budget-friendly activities like picnics or trips to discount stores can create lasting memories. The key is to prioritize thoughtful planning and creative ways to stretch your resources, which will teach your children the value of money and the importance of making the most of what you have. Always focus on the moments, not the money spent.

Diamond Moment

My belief in showing good stewardship revolves around managing your finances wisely and responsibly.

I continue to build my endurance by being consistent in the gym

Affirmations

Death and life are in the power of the tongue, and they that love it shall eat the fruit thereof.
Proverbs 18:21 (KJV)

We can speak words of prosperity and abundance into our lives. Our words have the ability to shape our reality and align us with God's purpose for us. Affirmations are positive declarative statements with motivating words that promote self-confidence, motivation, and personal growth. When repeated regularly, they can reinforce beliefs and nurture a positive mindset. Just as diamonds and pearls reveal their brilliance, affirmations help to refine and shape our thinking. They are instrumental in uncovering our inner strengths and potential. Affirmations serve as a mind shift from negative thoughts to thoughts of positivity that enable us to reduce anxiety and improve our ability to manage challenges effectively.

One way I initiate affirmations is by starting my morning routine with Bible scriptures that inspire me and set an uplifted mood throughout the day.

Managing tasks such as work, shopping, household chores, and navigating through traffic can get overwhelming. Beginning with an affirmation like "I will approach each task with clarity, quality, and purpose" increases my productivity and makes the tasks manageable while building a resilient mentality. This also enables me to train my brain to engage in uplifting thoughts rooted in faith and optimism.

My role as a realtor and active participant in several organizations involves regular driving to meetings and showing appointments. A few years ago, I experienced a severe episode of vertigo—a sensation of spinning or dizziness that feels as though you or your surroundings are moving or rotating. This episode resulted in intense anxiety during long-distance driving. However, I've learned to persevere through these moments by focusing on the scriptures.

"For God hath not given us the spirit of fear; but of power, and of love, and of sound mind."
2 Timothy 1:7 (KJV)

I also draw strength from a scripture my daughter Amber frequently shares:

"Nay, in all these things we are more than conquerors through him that loved us."

Romans 8:37 (KJV)

This scripture inspired me to create a powerful affirmation: *"I am more than an over-comer."*

Despite facing financial hardships, navigating through domestic challenges, and enduring health issues, I have remained resilient. My steadfast determination, faith, and positivity have transformed these obstacles into stepping stones, elevating me toward a more empowered version of myself.

Another source of affirmation comes from observing positive role models whose integrity and authenticity exemplify the power of optimism. Amid my son Clifton's graduation activities, as he received his Doctor of Musical Arts from Louisiana State University, we accompanied him to the campus bookstore to return his graduation regalia. We all committed to purchasing a keepsake to commemorate his milestone. After looking at all the souvenirs, I decided to buy a book because I felt this would offer ongoing value and inspiration. Trusting my instincts, I made my way to the book aisle, where I spotted the autobiography by my muse, former First Lady Michelle Obama. The book *Becoming* is a memoir of her life, describing a compelling story full of commitment and resilience that deeply resonated with me. I can relate to her challenges as an African American woman, residing close to her family and facing financial obstacles. I can only imagine the continual affirmations she had to cultivate.

Her documentary was a brilliant way to promote her book. I was impressed by how she interacted with a group of diverse women by engaging in an uplifting interview that included a question-and-answer session. When she asked each participant, "What are you becoming?" I saw an opportunity to claim an affirmation by asking myself, "What am I becoming?"

I am becoming resilient and stronger as I recover from difficult situations.

I am becoming optimistic about walking into my destiny and acknowledging my identity.

The thought of acknowledging my identity and becoming the best version of myself sparked a reflection on Maslow's theory of self-actualization, which explains the highest level of realizing your full potential and a deep sense of satisfaction.

My starting point was to consider the significance of my name, as it can reflect uniqueness, cultural heritage, and a sense of belonging. The name Elaine comes from the Greek origin, meaning "torch" or "shining light," and is believed to have originated from the name Helene. The biblical name Eli'anah, a similar Hebrew name, means "God has answered." My middle name, Francine, is derived from the Latin name "Francisca," which means "free one." This name often conveys a sense of freedom and elegance. As I explored these meanings, a surge of emotional energy inspired me to discover more effective ways to let my inner light shine with elegance, understanding, and purpose.

"Thy word is a lamp unto my feet, and a light unto my path."
Psalm 119:105 (KJV)

As I continue to seek my identity, I embrace the guidance of God's word with the ability to persevere through darkness. I pledge to allow my light to shine by demonstrating dedication, empathy, and excellence in all my endeavors.

Have you ever explored the significance of your name? What insights might it reveal about your identity? Names in biblical times were deeply significant because they intertwined with spiritual and cultural identity. Your name can serve as a foundation for acknowledging your heritage and creating affirmations that align with your values. This also aids in setting meaningful goals for growth and recognizing your strengths and talents.

Achieving long-term goals requires stronger affirmations that build perseverance and patience. Long-term generally refers to a period extending over a long duration, typically several years or more. Transforming diamonds and pearls is similar to long-term goals because they require time, patience, and gradual development. Both involve navigating obstacles and developing something valuable. Embracing goals or objectives means understanding they aren't always attained overnight but through consistency. The journey may be gradual, but it's worth the wait.

"But they that wait on the Lord shall renew their strength; they shall mount up with wings as eagles; they shall run, and not be weary, and they shall walk, and not faint."
Isaiah 40:31 (KJV)

A few examples of long-term goals are career advancement, financial security, personal development, and home ownership. These goals typically require years of strategic planning and dedication to achieve. One of my long-term goals is to become a landlord/entrepreneur, honoring my grandfather's legacy by merging my real estate experience with business management skills. To accomplish this, I continue to register for educational courses, including Toastmasters classes, actively networking, and joining several organizations.

My affirmation for this is: *"I can visualize my success, and I'm confident that this goal will manifest in time."*

On Sundays after church, I continue the tradition of visiting my mom's property—now an empty lot—which was passed down to her by her father and has since been passed down to me. I park at the front curb, pick up any trash, and walk through the yard, placing "No Trespassing" signs while visualizing and praying over the future construction of a multi-family unit. I ask God to guide this project and ensure it uplifts someone's life.

In addition, using vision boards helps reinforce my affirmations by displaying images and words that align with my desires. Recently, I've enhanced my board by incorporating elaborate backgrounds featuring African fabrics that highlight my aesthetic. The board was thoughtfully organized with affirmations for each section, such as "I'm creating an impact in the community" for my section on investment properties, "I will succeed in writing a captivating book" for becoming an author, and "Designs that shine with creativity" for my fashion aspiration. This yearly vision board is a powerful tool that incorporates visualizations, affirmations, and progress tracking in the goal-setting process.

Another long-term goal is to establish a secure retirement portfolio, which requires planning and self-discipline. My affirmation for this is: "I'm committed and capable of securing financial retirement assets." Maintaining consistency in investments, commissions, budgeting, and optimizing fixed-income expenses has proven an effective approach to building a resilient financial portfolio.

When I took a part-time job at Walmart, I considered it a temporary means to supplement my finances. However, it became more than that as I realized it had long-term advantages. Over the years, consistent payroll deductions for Walmart stock allowed me to accumulate a substantial investment that increased in value. Despite facing multiple financial hardships that pressured me to sell some shares, I remained unwavering in my commitment to maintain most of my investment. After many years, its value has grown substantially and continues to increase. Certain affirmations have the power to inspire and motivate others.

Homeownership was another memorable, long-term, life-changing goal that transformed my future. This required a strong affirmation, "I am confidently taking steps to move closer towards home ownership." As a determined young African American single parent of four, I aspired to become a homeowner despite all the naysayers. One evening as I was working my 12-hour shift at Compaq Computers, one of the ladies told of a first-time home buyer assistance program. With thankfulness and enthusiasm, I was excited to reveal I qualified for the program. I diligently followed all the instructions for pre-approval, which included taking a series of homeownership classes. After several hours of sacrifice and maneuvering through my demanding schedule, my dedication and perseverance were rewarded with the achievement of becoming a homeowner. My children radiated with joy as they eagerly personalized their new space. This blessing is a testament to the power of affirmations, demonstrating how they can provide reassurance and support.

"She maketh fine linen, and selleth it; and delivereth girdles unto the merchant. Strength and honor are her clothing, and she shall rejoice in time to come. She opened her mouth with wisdom, and in her tongue is the law of kindness. She looketh well to the ways of her household, and eateth not the bread of idleness. Her children arise up and call her blessed; her husband also, and he praiseth her."

Proverbs 31: 24-28 (KJV)

Diamond Moment

Embracing positive affirmations consistently empowers us to transform our mindset, by overcoming doubt so our full potential can emerge.

Sheila Jackson Lee (L) pictured with Elaine Moody (R)

I am a queen, and I demand to be treated like a queen.

— Sheila Jackson Lee

Reassurance

Chapter Four

"When thou passest through the waters, I will be with thee; and through the rivers, they shall not overflow thee: when thou walkest through the fire, thou shall not be burned; neither shall the flame kindle upon thee". Isaiah 43:2 (KJV)

It's time to talk about the power of reassurance. Reassurance is a gentle reminder of the support around us, offering comfort and strength during uncertain times. It provides the necessary support to navigate and endure challenges, just as diamonds and pearls rely on specific conditions in their formative stages.

Reassurance can manifest as an inner voice reminding you that you have support, and the strength to overcome obstacles that lie ahead. This provides comfort by easing anxiety and fear, validating feelings, and boosting self-assurance.

Did you know reassurance comes in different forms?

1. Emotional Reassurance
2. Informational Reassurance
3. Behavioral Reassurance
4. Practical Reassurance
5. Social Reassurance

Emotional Reassurance

My concept of emotional reassurance includes active listening, verbal affirmations, and understanding. A great example of this is the reassurance my best friend Linda Devenport offered during my stressful time of preparing for a promotion. I greatly appreciate the blessing of having her long-lasting and enduring friendship for over 60 years. Do you have a true and loyal lifetime friend? Our deep conversations, which sometimes lasted for hours, allowed us to actively listen to each other's trials and tribulations to offer support. Many treasured moments come to mind, especially those spent on her patio, where we contemplated optimistic possibilities for progress in our career paths.

During my tenure at the Texas Department of Public Safety (Driver License Division), I had the opportunity to be promoted to a higher position, which required several extensive exams and interviews. Linda was an invaluable source of support throughout the process. She helped me study for several weeks with flashcards during our travels to various places. Her encouragement consistently reassured me, saying "You've ready, You've got this". Thanks to her support and belief in me, I passed the tests and obtained the position. We vowed to stick together and raise our children in a godly way. I got gratification just listening to her voicemail greeting that said:

"The Lord is my light and my salvation; whom shall I fear? The Lord is the strength of my life; of whom shall I be afraid? When the wicked, even mine enemies and my foes, came upon me to eat up my flesh, they stumbled and fell."

Psalm 27:1-2 (KJV)

Informational Reassurance

Informational reassurance involves providing specific information or facts that help alleviate fear. It includes clear communication, consistency, and accuracy. An example would be explaining the steps involved in a process or providing detailed information about a situation. This is pivotal in addressing medical issues by providing patients with clear, accurate information about their condition, treatment options, and expectations.

My doctor informed me that I'm a borderline diabetic and knowing that diabetes runs in my family has prompted me to be more attentive to his recommendations. My focus is on learning preventive measures to improve my health, which is similar to cultivating diamonds and pearls because both require consistent care and the right conditions to thrive. Regular consultations help me prioritize screenings, lab work, and maintaining a proper diet. During Diabetes Awareness Month in November, many health organizations and hospitals promoted workshops full of resources to raise awareness and obtain management strategies. I've adjusted to alternative cooking techniques to encourage better eating habits while enjoying flavorful foods. Barbecuing, grilling, or baking chicken breasts paired with roasted or steamed vegetables can be very tasty. Adapting to a specialized diet has reassured me that it can improve and sustain my good health.

A critical health crisis for the nation was the COVID-19 pandemic, officially recognized in March 2020. Dr. Fauci, Director of the National Institute of Allergy and Infectious Diseases (NIAID) played a significant role in providing the nation with expert advice and solutions through the media. A lot of panic and turmoil was reduced due to his informative reassurance. It created a new normal which included a six-foot rule, masks, temperature checks, and cancellations of many social gatherings. First responders and essential workers were critical parts of our safety and well-being. Utilizing Zoom, Google Meet, Door Dash, and

Curbside pickup options changed how we worked, shopped, and studied. Government mandates imposed school closures that resulted in remote learning programs. I became "Nana the Teacher" to my grandson Kamari as my home office was transformed into a classroom-like environment. I logged into Google Meet several times a day, starting with morning activities beginning with the Pledge of Allegiance followed by roll, announcements, and the daily schedule. The evening activities included reading and math. Initially, managing the curriculum was very overwhelming, but I gradually adjusted and the teacher reassured us that we were doing a great job. A year later, vaccines were discovered and administered, allowing several institutions to reopen cautiously.

Behavioral Reassurance

Behavioral reassurance involves gestures that offer comfort through supportive actions such as hugs, holding hands, and eye contact. Over time, I've become aware of the significant value of support and the sense of security from physical presence and interaction.

One of the most defining moments was discovering I was expecting my first child. How would you feel realizing you're about to become someone's mother? I was overjoyed to share this praise report with my mother, knowing that despite the miles apart, (she was in Houston, Texas and I lived in Clarksville, Tennessee) our bond remained stronger than ever. I could almost feel her hugs and see her smiles in my mind.

Her wisdom reassured me of my resilience as I navigated the muscle aches, anticipation, and apprehensions of pregnancy. Mom's constant support reminded me that I was stronger than I had ever realized. While talking with her one day, I mentioned the intense aches and pains I was experiencing even though it was still a couple of weeks before my due date. She immediately advised me to go to the hospital and be checked for labor. As always, she was right. Before being admitted, I was able to call her and share my feelings of nervousness about the process and the pain. Mom advised me to visualize her face on the doctor or nurse in the delivery room. This strategy worked, it felt as though she was physically there and providing me with the courage I needed. After enduring the pain of childbirth, my son Clifton was born, and I was blessed to become a mother, gifted with a precious baby. My mother's wise words continued to guide me through the pregnancies of my other children even though she was deceased I was reminded of the reassurance she provided. I used the same strategy to reassure my daughter Chanel as she faced a situation almost identical to mine. As she received the thrilling news of becoming a mom while living in Phoenix, Arizona, I was in Houston, Texas. My journey as a mother has been deeply enriched by the consistent behavioral reassurance I've both given and received from my family, creating a cycle of support and strength that has guided us all.

To support my grandson Kamari, I became actively involved in the Aldine Family and Community Engagement (FACE) program. My persistent devotion was acknowledged when the specialist, Mr. Ivan Tamayo, honored me by asking me to deliver the commencement speech at our annual graduation. The responsibility of giving an inspiring speech to such a large crowd resulted in countless hours of crafting the appropriate words that would resonate with my fellow graduates. After several rewrites and reading it repeatedly, doubts still lingered in my mind. On graduation day, I nervously approached the stage with shaking hands that clenched onto my speech. When gazing into the audience the sight of my daughter (Amber) and my husband (William) standing and waving, fueled me with so much reassurance and confidence that I began speaking before the microphone was turned on. The interpreter played a vital role in helping me deliver a meaningful speech, as I was instructed to pause throughout so she could translate it into Spanish. At the end of the speech, the audience applauded while several faculty members congratulated me on the heartfelt message.

"That their hearts might be comforted, being knit together in love, and unto all riches of full assurance of understanding, to the acknowledgment of the mystery of God, and of the Father, and of Christ; In whom are hid all the treasures of wisdom and knowledge".

Colossians 2:2-3 (KJV)

Providing reassurance fulfills the psychological needs that fuel our hopes and aspirations to overcome challenges and achieve more. This has propelled me to network with positive people who offer valuable connections and validation. Behavioral reassurance has developed me into an empowered individual who recognizes and embraces her unique values.

Practical Reassurance

Practical reassurance provides comfort through tangible actions by offering support that directly addresses fears in a clear and effective way. A definition could explain how practical reassurance might include offering detailed instructions on managing a task by providing necessary tools or outlining a clear plan. A clearer example would be instructions on assembling a bike or a book on personal development.

The Bible is my essential toolkit offering scriptures that provide comfort, guidance, and wisdom. These divine insights help me manage life's challenges and ease stress. I experienced a lot of pressure during my tenure at a customer service job due to jealousy, backstabbing, and cliches composed of long-tenured employees. Truthfully, I admit there have been times when I succumbed to the toxic environment. However, my actions were never so out of character as to warrant the rude treatment I received. Seeking comfort and guidance, I began reading the Bible and praying throughout the office daily.

But I say unto you, Love your enemies, bless them that curse you, do good to them that hate you and pray for them that despitefully use you and persecute you. Matthew 5:44 (KJV)

After a couple of years, the job went under significant changes which resulted in downsizing the staff and selling the building. Reading the Bible offered me reassurance that God heard and resolved my situation. I remembered my Pastor's challenge of reading the entire bible in 6 months. It felt impossible but I began listening to the audio version as my daily routine. I completed it in a year and started revisiting it repeatedly. Reading the Bible over

12 times has led to a deep emotional discovery of peace and joy. I've risen from a defenseless employee to a resilient entrepreneur.

Social Reassurance

Social reassurance refers to the emotional support we receive from others that uplifts our spirits and strengthens our sense of connection. Movies and songs are excellent examples of social reassurance because they resonate with shared experiences and emotions.

The movie "War Room" comes to mind as the character Elizabeth, a real estate agent is introduced to the concept of a dedicated space for prayer (war room) where she can fight her battles through prayer rather than arguments and anger. The movie shows how focused prayer can provide tangible results by offering reassurance that effectively transforms hardships into triumphs. Mandisa's song "Press On" in the film effectively embodies the theme of perseverance, much like her journey chronicled in her book "Out of the Dark". Her song and book resonate with the message that even in the most stressful times, faith and resilience can overcome adversity. The film emphasizes the power of strategic fervent prayer that highlights themes of forgiveness, faith, and spiritual warfare. Although her life was short-lived, the impact of her work will leave a legacy of inspiration.

Diamond Moment

Reassurance is the foundation for creating faith that leads to confidence and hope when things seem impossible. A little faith (mustard seed) goes a long way.

Reassurance comes not from the absence of struggle, but from knowing that you are never alone in it.

Living for a Legacy

"A good man leaveth an inheritance for his children's children, and the wealth of the sinner is laid up for the just."
Proverbs 13:22 (KJV)

My approach to establishing a great legacy is to create and instill family values that include lifestyles of love with goal-driven inspirations. The impactful "I Have a Dream" speech from Rev. Dr. Martin Luther King, Jr. resonates deeply with me. I was 10 years old when I heard the speech from the black-and-white television in our small shotgun house. Dr. King said, "Like anybody, I would like to live a long life. Longevity has its place. But I'm not concerned about that now. I just want to do God's will." His charismatic voice echoed through the massive audience as he delivered a speech of inspiring hope.

The following day, the shocking news of Rev. Dr. Martin Luther King Jr.'s assassination sent the entire country into a state of shock. His life's work of preaching, protesting, and marching was not in vain, as the long-lasting vision of advocating principles of equality is the foundation of some present-day regulations.

Parades, speeches, streets, and a holiday named in his honor are tributes to his legacy and influence. His speeches gave me the inspiration and commitment to become an advocate for those ostracized from society because of racial, financial, physical, and civil status.

As I grew into my season of deeper gratitude and humbleness, I began to ponder, possess, and proclaim his same passion: "I just want to do God's will." My mission is to be a worthy vessel that will make a lasting impact on society by setting a positive example and initiating community service. The pledge to produce a better version of myself triggered a challenge for personal development while acquiring a sense of duty to inspire others to embrace their strengths and talents.

After reading the book *Purpose Driven Life* by Rick Warren, I discovered that true fulfillment comes from developing a deeper spiritual growth that creates a sense of belonging, which is the third level of Maslow's pyramid.

Connecting with like-minded groups gives me a strong sense of purpose because it can lead to actions and goals that create a lasting impact. I find fulfillment by engaging with volunteering groups for community service while collaborating with professionals on business activities. I pledge to dig deeper to discover the gifts God has given me to manifest my purpose and create a lasting mark of influence. Like some diamonds and pearls are traditionally passed down from generation to generation as family heirlooms, legacies involve passing on values and wisdom.

It's an esteemed honor and privilege to carry on the legacy of my Aunt Mildred by consistently participating in the Mildred Johnson Juneteenth Pageant. This allows me to continue her legacy of encouraging excellence in etiquette. Each year, the pageant is dedicated to guiding and elevating young ladies and now young men by providing teaching and training to exhibit their talents and engage in public speaking. This annual Juneteenth event honors the historical legacy of African Americans who received the announcement of emancipation in Texas on June 19, 1865, nearly two and a half years after the Emancipation Proclamation was issued on January 1, 1863, which marked the official end of slavery in the United States. Not only is this the liberation of enslaved individuals, but also the ongoing journey towards justice and equality.

Building on principles of equality strengthened me to promote inclusivity in all my interactions to ensure essential ethics are displayed. I realize how blessed I am to have a strong foundation from my parents, grandparents, and other family members. The kindness they showed to the community is still remembered by many who look to me to maintain their values.

"And the things that thou hast heard of me among many witnesses, the same commit thou to faithful men, who shall be able to teach others also." 2 Timothy 2:2 (KJV)

My goal in life is to contribute something meaningful to society by inspiring others. Virtues can become the building blocks for legacies because they define our character by producing principles that transcend to future generations. My need to succeed is fueled by faith and patience in all I do. Patience is a guiding virtue that allows me to develop gradually over time with a unique value that I compare to diamonds and pearls.

Singles Setting a Legacy

During my teenage years in the 1970s, society's traditional expectation was that a young man and woman would marry their soul mate around 20 or 30 years old. Singles are no longer tethered by society's conventional trends toward marriage. The new perspective of marriage as a choice rather than a necessity has compelled this new generation to prioritize their independence before committing to marriage. They've learned to focus on career goals and discovering their identity.

Shifting narratives in books and movies that showcase single life in a positive light helps singles embrace their independence. I enjoyed watching a TV show in the early '90s called *Living Single.* The comedy show revolved around six independent African American singles, four women and two men with professional careers in Brooklyn, New York. They exhibited positive problem-solving as they navigated their careers and relationships. As I think about prominent single African American women, iconic trailblazers like Oprah Winfrey and Condoleezza Rice come to mind. Their **P**erseverance, **E**mpowerment, **A**ccountability, and **R**esilience establish **L**egacies that expand beyond their professional achievements. As a fellow baby boomer, I treasure the pearls of wisdom these phenomenal women have shared.

Single Parents: A Lifestyle of Strength, Sacrifice and Resilience

Most people try to avoid the status of becoming a single parent. Key factors such as incompatibility, generational patterns, and becoming a widow often led individuals to choose this lifestyle. Research suggests some women, like myself, stay in a relationship or marriage for the sake of the kids or financial security. Neither of these reasons justifies staying in a toxic relationship, as it can lead to long-term stress and strain. Do you know anyone who seems to be in a relationship filled with more pressure than pleasure?

Despite the much-appreciated support from their fathers, my family, and friends, there were many days when my situation felt overwhelming. For over 13 years as a single African American parent, I encountered numerous challenges that included economic, emotional, and purpose-driven obstacles, but I persevered. Similar to the pressures that develop diamonds and pearls, the hardships and heartaches I endured transformed me into the quality-driven person I am today. I attribute most of it to my spiritual growth. Succeeding requires faith, courage, sacrifice, selflessness, confidence, and patience.

During tough times, I would look at my kids as they slept, lay hands on them, and pray for guidance in providing a better future for us. As soon as I started to pray, memories of my grandmother's prayers flooded my mind. I vividly remember her sitting in a designated chair in the corner of her living room, reciting prayers that still resound in my ears, "Lord, you made us, and you know all about us." My prayers always started acknowledging God's divine presence and ended with gratitude, thanking him for his grace and mercy. I continue to pray for them today, earnestly asking:

Dear Lord, thank you for blessing us on this day, and please surround my children with your protection and love. Help them grow in wisdom and understanding to follow the path of righteousness. Heavenly Father, please fill their hearts with resilience to overcome difficulties and bless them with good health. Please fill their lives with positive relationships and allow them to feel loved, valued, and supported. I honor you with praise for your endless blessings. In the mighty name of Jesus, I pray, Amen.

The power of prayer has been a driving force that has guided our family through many generations, providing us with countless blessings, healing, protection, and a strong faith that has enabled us to overcome challenges.

Living Happily Married

Marriage is one of the most celebrated milestones in life because it signifies an alliance of love with a commitment to sharing a lifelong union with your soul mate. A resilient and affectionate marriage can convey valuable lessons to children, grandchildren, and the community that leave a lasting impact. It was always a delight to visit my Aunt Mildred (Lady "J") and Uncle George (Rev. Johnson, my dad's brother) because I viewed them as a powerful couple who inspired many people. They were well known for their stylish and coordinated attire, which they wore to most events. Children from Uncle George's organization, Divine Dynasty, looked forward to summer camp visits to Bronson, Missouri, where they would unite with a larger organization, Kids Across America. The young ladies from Aunt Mildred's group, the Charmettes, were always excited about performing at social events and eager to explore diverse cultures and luxurious lifestyles.

Aunt Mildred and Uncle George's collective efforts not only inspired multiple generations, but through their legendary mentorship, they've inspired so many kids to rise above the struggles and stereotypes associated with their humble beginnings. This paved the way for a brighter future. The heartfelt testimonies from those they mentored serve as a reminder that their efforts were meaningful and not in vain. The positive impact of their teamwork as a married couple extended beyond their families and touched the lives of the entire community.

Faithful Inheritance

Faith is a powerful legacy that originated throughout the Bible with patriarchs, prophets, and kings. There's true validation that faith has been inherited through generations in my family and my husband's. My most direct witness to dedicated acts of faith was observing how my mother performed what felt like a "mission impossible." With her modest income, she made sure we had the resources to participate in extracurricular activities like band, cosmetology, and social clubs. I vividly remember her happily doing household chores while humming, "I Will Trust in the Lord," and this has left a lasting impression on me. I often find myself doing the same thing. My father-in-law, Mr. Warren G. Hardy Moody Sr., led by example in being a man of integrity and trust. This utilization of teachable moments has provided the groundwork of faith for several generations.

As you reflect on the importance of legacy, remember that the values you build today will serve as the foundation for future generations. Whether through acts of kindness, a commitment to faith, or simply leading a life of integrity, your legacy extends beyond material wealth. It lives on in the people you've impacted and the lessons you've imparted. Focus on leaving behind principles that uplift and inspire, knowing that the love and guidance you offer will echo far beyond your lifetime and shape the futures of those who follow.

Creating a positive legacy can involve embodying resilience as a single parent, embracing the virtues of a strong marriage, and passing down a faith-based lifestyle.

Elaine Moody and Family

An inheritance is what you leave with people. A legacy is what you leave in them

Success

"Keep this Book of the Law always on your lips; meditate on it day and night, so that you may be careful to do everything written in it. Then you will be prosperous and successful."
Joshua 1:8 (KJV)

The essence of success embodies different meanings to everyone and can vary depending on goals and ambitions. Maintaining consistency and adapting to external factors such as industry trends and economic conditions can pave the way to financial success. My definition of success means maintaining integrity, pursuing my purpose, and finding fulfillment in personal development. This empowers me to create a plan that elevates my purpose and prosperity to a higher level. A quote that has great significance to me is:

"Success is liking yourself, liking what you do, and liking how you do it."

- Mayou Angelou

As I arrived in the parking lot of Dress for Success, a 501(c)(3) non-profit organization, to complete my community service hours, I was immediately impressed by the beautiful glass building with modern architectural design. Upon entering the upscale, elaborately decorated foyer, the receptionist greeted me warmly and directed me to the sign-in area to receive my badge. A guide then led me to a classroom for orientation.

During the PowerPoint presentation that explained how we would assist applicants with proper attire, resume writing, and personal hygiene, my mind wandered in another direction. When hearing the phrase "Dress for Success," the perception of a power suit or business attire is the first thing that comes to mind. However, a well-poised appearance is only part of the picture; proper heart and soul preparation is equally important.

Wherefore take unto you the whole armor of God that ye may be able to withstand in the evil day, and having done all, to stand. Stand, therefore, having your loins girt about with truth, and having on the breastplate of righteousness; And your feet shod with the preparation of the gospel of peace; Above all, taking the shield of faith, wherewith ye shall be able to quench all the fiery darts of the wicked. And take the helmet of salvation, and the sword of the spirit, which is the word of God: Praying always with all prayer and supplication in the Spirit, and watching thereunto with all perseverance and supplication for all saints: Ephesians 6:13-18 (KJV)

This scripture illustrates an analogy of how the whole armor of God shields the heart and soul against spiritual warfare, allowing prosperity to manifest. The belt of truth is a fundamental element that binds core virtues to foster personal development and guide one toward achieving the fullest potential. It equips me with the tools to conduct ethical behavior, enhancing my credibility to elevate quality service. I aspire to consistently promote loyalty that cultivates positive networking for sustaining professional growth. The elements of the armor of God work together to nurture a strong, sincere servant who delights in performing good works that can spread positivity and counteract negativity.

There's significant value in delivering exceptional customer service. As a former customer service representative at Wal-Mart, my challenge was providing the highest level of service for numerous requests simultaneously. These services included handling returns and exchanges, processing money orders, and making announcements for lost children in the store, among others. Whether the customers were polite or rude, the company expected me to maintain courtesy to uphold their previous motto: "Satisfaction guaranteed."

The back of our vests read, "How May I Help You?" This marketing strategy exemplifies customer assistance. It effectively communicates the employee's commitment to providing quality service with a proactive approach to customer interaction. This simple yet impactful message serves as brilliant advertising. Ultimately, developing great character, regardless of the type of job, is a cornerstone for personal and professional success.

In both personal and professional settings, being a great servant involves sincere empathy that encompasses going the extra mile with commitment and compassion. How does it make you feel when someone takes the time to accompany you through the store to ensure you find what you're looking for instead of just giving directions or pointing down the aisle? I feel valued and grateful.

The purpose of the breastplate of righteousness is to protect the heart by initiating an inspiration to forgive and eradicate prolonged anger, jealousy, and revenge. I began to see things with a new mindset that allowed me to respond with poise versus persecution. Throughout my corporate career, there have been numerous instances when it became necessary to forgive the acts of overly ambitious employees by remembering to work as if I were "working for the Lord."

"And whatsoever ye do, do it heartily, as to the Lord, and not unto men."

Colossians 3:23 (KJV)

Your shoes, symbolizing the gospel of peace, provide stability for spiritual readiness and eagerness to share the good news of salvation. Divine instructions lead and direct me when to stand patiently or when to proceed with boldness. I often think about the phrase, "Before you judge me, walk a mile in my shoes." This encourages me to consider other's situations and approach them with empathy and compassion.

There've been times when I reacted negatively without first contemplating the possibility of serious underlying issues. One day, I was late for an event and became frustrated with heavy traffic and the driver in front of me. Angrily passing in the next lane, I soon realized it was a senior citizen experiencing health issues. This resonated with me because of my episode with vertigo while driving. I immediately felt a sense of shame and conviction for my initial reaction and began to pray for the driver.

Wielding the shield of faith enables me to trust in my potential for success. It empowers me with the strength and bandwidth to seize profitable opportunities. I believe the effective utilization of faith is the glue that holds trust and potential possibilities together. The helmet of salvation and the sword of the spirit—the Word of God—offer wisdom, clarity, and problem-solving skills that help me navigate challenges in my career as a real estate and life insurance agent. When I meet a client for the first time, my utmost priority is to assure them of my commitment to delivering the highest level of service while guiding them throughout the process.

In my early years as a real estate agent, this journey was quite intimidating. I worked through my nervousness by consulting experienced professionals to ensure accuracy. I've always felt a responsibility to be transparent with my clients regarding uncertainties by pledging to verify information from trusted sources. These experiences inspired me to take several courses to earn designations that enabled me to acquire knowledge that resulted in higher self-confidence.

The most valuable treasure I've discovered on my journey to success is how it has shaped me into the person I was destined to become. Success is also about deep connections, sharing knowledge, and experiencing happiness in discovering a true sense of self-actualization which is the top tier in Maslow's hierarchy of needs. As I celebrate my season of self-worth, the transformation of a shy and reserved woman has evolved into a confident professional. A valuable lesson learned is that challenges can create opportunities for personal growth and prosperity. Endurance of the trials of life has shaped me into a resilient individual, radiating inner and outer beauty like diamonds and pearls. Whenever I interact with the public, whether face to face or on social media, others see my personality as an uplifting delight that benefits those around me.

Diamond Moment

Meeting talented and uplifting colleagues is a treasure. We encourage each other to become high achievers. All things work together to produce successes that create a positive change.

Say Yes to the Process

Treasure

Treasures are often classified as a collection of valuable items like diamonds, pearls, gold, money, or other tangible items that symbolize great wealth and are usually hidden or stored away. Classic movies like *Treasure Island* or *Indiana Jones and the Last Crusade* illustrate the suspenseful journey of a pirate seeking to find a treasure with an action-packed adventure. Both movies involve deciphering clues, outsmarting rivals, and overcoming challenges. The scenario usually depicts the pirate (treasure seeker) as a fearless leader with a rugged appearance.

The strategies pirates use to search for treasures are similar to how we navigate life by seeking pearls of wisdom, joy, and fulfillment. Just like pirates follow clues, we follow instincts, opportunities, and testimonies to discover the treasures in our lives. I consider the teachings of my mother, Aunt Mildred, grandparents, and lessons at church as invaluable treasures that have enriched my life. They define who I am and cultivate an emotional balance by helping me stay grounded while alleviating feelings of anxiety.

My mother, a woman full of faith and wisdom, stressed the importance of a clean home with a peaceful environment full of love and peace. Before we went to school, our beds were always made, clothes were hung, making sure the kitchen and bathroom were clean. This carried over into my adult life as I realized a clean and organized home would provide an atmosphere that cultivates a clean heart and mind. I continue to experience feelings of calmness when I enter my clean home after a long stressful day.

My Aunt Mildred, a trailblazer in the community, always exhibited elegance not only in her attire but in her etiquette also. She taught proper greetings, dress, and table manners. I watched how she patiently taught young children how to interact with others. My favorite memories were listening to her calm and articulate voice as she spoke. She taught that *true etiquette isn't about showing off; it's about being confident about who you are and showing others the same respect you want to receive.* As I grew older, I realized these valuable lessons were essential in almost every aspect of the customer service industry.

My exposure to spiritual teachings at Bella Vista Missionary Baptist Church at a young age was a road map to obtaining the key to perseverance. It instilled in me the values of faith, resilience, and patience during challenging times in my life. Investing in my spiritual growth has brought me significant value by equipping me with salvation for eternal life.

"But the fruit of the Spirit is love, joy, peace, longsuffering, gentleness, goodness, faith…"

Galatians 5:22 (KJV)

I've adopted a lifestyle focused on dedicating my time to spreading goodwill. Acts of kindness such as holding the door for a senior citizen, offering a small donation to the homeless, or even letting someone with fewer items go ahead of me in line at the grocery store bring me joy. These actions enrich our lives and create an environment of compassion in our homes, churches, and communities.

Years ago, at the end of our church service, Pastor Abraham would always ask us to repeat a statement: "I ain't got nothing of lasting value if I don't have Jesus. But I've got him, he's in me, and I'm in him." Although Pastor Abraham is no longer with us, this statement is invaluable. Have you contemplated the abundance of treasures you have?

I perceive time as a treasured commodity because it shapes our lives with experiences that create testimonies. My husband and kids always ask what I want on special occasions like my birthday, Mother's Day, Christmas, and anniversaries. Throughout the years, I've acquired so many material things that have eventually become worn, broken, and some even lost. My most treasured gifts are the times that I spend with family. I enjoy family fish fries, watching my son Clifton direct the UT-Austin Longhorn band, and I always look forward to my daughter Chanel's visits from Arizona with my grandson Christian. The daily routine with my grandson Kamari is also a joy. My son Jakari is always willing to help me and my husband with various tasks.

    One Mother's Day, my daughter Amber took me to a high tea at a fancy restaurant in Downtown Houston. After valet parking, we entered the elaborately decorated area, where a greeter escorted us to our table. We were dressed in our high tea attire, complete with fancy hats and gloves matching our dresses. Our etiquette came naturally but was certainly noticeable throughout the restaurant. We were treated like royalty, which made me feel like a treasured diamond.

So many cherished memories of my children and grandchildren have brought me immeasurable joy. Unlike material possessions, time cannot be bought, saved, or recovered. I see this treasure as an opportunity to make important choices. By investing wisely in personal development and pursuing passions by networking with others, I can enrich our lives while contributing to our well-being.

I consider writing this book a treasure because it taught me endurance and perseverance throughout this journey. The support and patience of Ms. Ebony Rose, who believed in me and continuously boosted my confidence, was priceless.

"Let perseverance finish its work so that you may be mature and complete, not lacking anything."

James 1:4 (NIV)

We have spiritual treasures that the world can't take away.

Under Pressure

Pressure

"We are hard pressed on every side, but not crushed; perplexed, but not in despair; persecuted, but not abandoned; struck down but not destroyed."

2 Corinthians 4:8-9 (NIV)

Pressure may appear negative, but it can lead to positive change if applied with a constructive objective. Both physical and mental pressures serve as powerful tools for transformation into an elevated state. One example that relates to physical pressure is the process of childbirth. I have given birth to four children through various delivery methods, including natural, anesthesia-assisted, and C-section, and I experienced the pressure of labor pains with each one. Labor pains occur because the baby's movement down the birth canal puts pressure on the mother's body, causing contractions. As I held my newborns, the joy of giving life put the pain and pressure into perspective. To those who are mothers, how did you feel after the delivery of your baby? Another example of physical pressure is the weight applied to a wound to control blood loss or chest compression to restore blood flow to vital organs. When properly administered, this facilitates healing.

An example of mental pressure is experiencing financial challenges and life-changing circumstances that become overwhelming, creating constant worry, uncertainty, and emotional strain. Using spiritual precepts can activate a survival mode that allows us to overcome these pressures by enhancing our endurance. The three invaluable principles that kept me grounded and helped maintain my sanity are *faith, belief, and dream.* For many years, I wrote these words on the top margin of each page of my journal. As I focused on each word, I took time to process them individually.

Faith instills hope and encouragement, strengthening my assurance that God is always there to help me persevere through life's pressures. **Belief supplies** the resilience I need to bounce back from adversities by trusting that all things work together for my good. **Dreams** supply me with positive visions, reminding me that God has provided everything I need to prosper. Dreams also bring hope that there is a brighter day ahead. These three words have proven to be my secret source of elevation when life's pressures weigh me down.

"Now faith is the substance of things hoped for, and the evidence of things not seen."

Hebrews 11:1 (KJV)

Handling financial obligations as a single parent put an enormous amount of pressure on me. Meeting basic needs like food, shelter, and healthcare generated pressures that contributed to a surmounting level of anxiety. I've been blessed to receive child support, which helped considerably. However, I still needed to work additional jobs to create multiple streams of income. Juggling these jobs to meet my financial needs revealed my resourcefulness and demonstrated my resilience as a true survivor.

Did you know that peer pressure can work for and against you? It's important to surround yourself with the right peers. My fitness journey involves pressures, both physical and mental. Seeing others at the gym push through intense routines challenges me to stretch beyond my limits. While this inspires me to challenge myself, it also reminds me to focus on progressing at my own pace. I've come to realize that it's not just the number on the scale that matters but rather a consistent commitment to a health regimen. Understanding your tolerance level is a significant cornerstone for navigating life's pressures.

The pressure of losing a loved one can have a deeper impact on some individuals, potentially leading to major depression, depending on your mindset. My sisters and I faced the death of my mother as young adults, and my sister Rebecca, who was born through the union of my Dad's remarriage, faced the bereavement of her mom as a young teenager. We rose above this life-changing situation by receiving support from our family. Despite Rebecca's situation, she navigated her grief with grace and became a remarkable young lady—a testament to the power of perseverance and faith.

The inspiring Bible story about Job provides an example of steadfast faith and belief during times of extreme pressures of wealth, health, and personal loss. Job experienced all these forms of pressure within a few days. Throughout these hardships, he remained steadfast while maintaining his integrity. Job was a wealthy and righteous man who faithfully served God. God allowed Satan to test Job by taking away his wealth, health, and children to see if he would remain faithful. Although Job questioned why he was experiencing these pressures, he maintained his belief in God's sovereignty. His faithfulness was rewarded when God restored his health, increased his wealth, and blessed him with more children. This story illustrates how the belief that faith can lead to restoration if you persevere through life's pressures.

"Though he slay me, yet will I trust in him; but I will maintain mine own ways before him."

Job 13:15 (KJV)

After prayer and supplication to address stress, I immerse myself in hobbies that bring me to a relaxed state of mind. Creating garments or working in my garden fills me with a sense of peacefulness. When I sit with the ladies in my knitting class, we share experiences that inspire positive solutions and reduce unnecessary pressures. Have you ever engaged in hobbies like painting, sewing, gardening, or puzzles to take your mind off of troubles? Consistency in nurturing hobbies can unlock hidden talents to reveal your true gifts and treasures. Persevering under pressure strengthens resilience and brings you closer to success.

Diamond Moment

Regardless of the pressures we face, our steadfast trust in God gives us the victory to persevere through them.

Acknowledgments

Most of the scriptural references in this book are from the Bible, specifically the King James Version and the New International Version. The book also references Maslow's hierarchy of needs. The biblical teachings and preaching from my church, Bella Vista Missionary Baptist Church, under the pastoral leadership of Dr. Jacari P. Davis and the late Pastor Calvin J. Abraham, significantly inspired this book. I express my heartfelt gratitude to my publisher, Ebony Rose, and my dear friend/classmate, Ms. Dorothy Jenkins. Their unwavering compassion was essential to my perseverance in completing this book. Thank you for believing in me and encouraging me every step of the way.

About the Author

Elaine Moody is a uniquely designed woman gifted with many talents that allow her to prosper mentally and financially. As a devoted wife, mother of four, and grandmother to two energetic little boys, she is committed to being the best version of herself. Earning a bachelor's degree in business administration has given her the confidence to obtain her licenses in real estate, life insurance, and providing notary public services. Her mission is to use her knowledge to uplift others through personal testimonies and motivational speaking.

www.ingramcontent.com/pod-product-compliance
Ingram Content Group UK Ltd.
Pitfield, Milton Keynes, MK11 3LW, UK
UKHW021310180426
11947UKWH00015B/1135